Just the Facts

Tuberculosis

Kristina Routh

Heinemann Library
Chicago, Illinois

Customer Service 888-454-2279
Visit our website at www.heinemannlibrary.com

Produced by Monkey Puzzle Media
Designed by Jane Hawkins
Originated by Ambassador Litho Ltd.
Consultant: Jane Bullen, TB nurse, Brighton General Hospital
Printed and bound in China by South China Printing Company

08 07 06 05 04
10 9 8 7 6 5 4 3 2 1

Library of Congress Cataloging-in-Publication Data
A copy of the cataloging-in-publication data for this title is on file with the Library of Congress.
Tuberculosis/ Kristina Routh
ISBN 1-4034-5147-8

Acknowledgments
The publishers would like to thank the following for permission to reproduce photographs: Alamy pp. 19 (John Powell), 32 (Photofusion); Corbis pp. 12 (Ronnie Kaufmann), 23 (Oksanentessa/Sygma), 39 (Wolfgang Kaehler); Hulton Archive p. 7; Mary Evans Picture Library p. 8; Network p. 28 (Jenny Matthews); Panos p. 13 (Gareth Jones); Press Association pp. 29 (EPA), 50 (EPA), 51 (EPA); Rex Features pp. 22 (West Australian Newspapers Ltd), 25 (SIPA), 44–45 (SIPA); Science Photo Library pp. 1 (BSIP/Laurent/Lesache), 4 (Horacio Sormani), 6, 11, 14 (BSIP/Laurent/Lesache), 16–17 (Horacio Sormani), 34 (Biophoto Associates), 35 (Will and Deni McIntryre), 36–37 (Mike Miller), 38 (NIBSC), 41 (A. Crump/TDR/WHO), 46–47 (Hattie Young), 48 (H. Raguet); Still Pictures pp. 26–27 (Roland Seitre), 31 (Shehzad Noorani); Stop TB Partnership p. 43 (Gary Hampton/TBP/WHO); Wellcome Trust pp. 9, 15. The map on pp. 20–21 is by Michael Posen.

The author and publishers would like to acknowledge Dr Graham Simpson, Director of the TB Control Unit at Cairns Base Hospital, North Queensland, Australia for the quote on p.22; Dr Jai Shakla-Lala, formerly of St Stephen's Hospital, Delhi for the case study on pp. 30–31; The North of Tyne Communicable Disease Control Unit, Newcastle Upon Tyne, UK for the quotes on pp. 12, 17, 33, 35, 39 and 44, and the case study on p. 19; The TB Elimination division for the Texas Department of Health, USA for the quotes on pp. 42 and 47; Heather Vogell of The Gotham Gazette.com website for the case study on p. 47.

Cover photograph: main image: Stop TB Partnership (WHO/ TBP/ Arnold); second image: Science Photo Library/ SIU/ Peter Arnold Inc.

Contents

Introducing Tuberculosis

Tuberculosis is one of the most damaging infectious diseases in the world. Around the globe, it kills over 2 million people a year, including more than 250,000 children. Usually known as TB, the disease is caused by tiny bacteria that can be passed from person to person just by breathing the same air.

Anyone can catch TB, but it thrives wherever humans live closely together in poor conditions. It is very common in many developing countries, especially where healthcare services are inadequate. It is also a big problem in parts of some developed countries where people still live in overcrowded conditions.

Doctors all over the world have to deal with the problem of TB, including here in Tibet.

Having TB

A person can be infected with TB without knowing it. The bacteria lie dormant (sleeping) in the lungs and, in some people, may break out later to cause disease. Approximately one-third of the world's population is infected with TB in this way.

Although it can develop in almost any part of the body, TB usually affects the lungs. The effects may be severe. The infected person becomes thinner and thinner as the disease appears to consume, or eat up, the body.

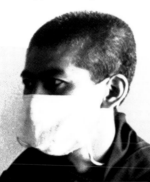

❝TB is one of the most seriously neglected and underestimated health, human rights, and poverty problems of our era.❞

(UNICEF, 2000)

A curable disease…

TB is nearly 100 percent curable if people take the right medicines for the correct length of time. Unfortunately, many people, particularly in developing countries, do not have access to the correct medicines, or cannot manage to take them for the many months that are needed. This means people still die of this curable disease.

…but still a problem

One hundred years ago, TB was very common in developed countries such as the United States and United Kingdom. Then better living conditions and effective antibiotics reduced the number of cases so dramatically that people in these countries thought that TB was a thing of the past.

However, over the last twenty years there has been a growth in TB in these countries as well as around the world. This is partly due to the rise in HIV infection, with which it is often linked. People are beginning to realize that something needs to be done to improve the situation – and it needs to be done soon.

TB Through the Ages

TB is probably the largest single cause of death and disease in all of human history. We know that TB has been infecting humans for thousands of years. The earliest evidence of tuberculosis is from a Neolithic grave, near Heidelberg in Germany, dating back to 5000 B.C.E.

Egyptian mummies have been found from 4,000 years ago that show telltale signs of Pott's disease – TB within the bones of the spine. There are also 2,000-year-old writings from India describing tuberculosis as the "King of Diseases."

Industrialization and TB

TB has always been present in human communities, but it is most common where people live very closely together in poor conditions. Over the last few hundred years, as Europe became increasingly industrialized, many people left the countryside to work and live in large towns and cities. Living conditions were often cramped, with large families crowded together in small rooms. TB was able to spread easily.

This tracing from an ancient Egyptian tomb shows a man suffering from Pott's disease, or TB of the spine.

TB became a common and distressing cause of disease and death. By the 17th century, one in five deaths in London was due to TB. In the 19th century, TB became known as the White Plague. It took hold of the major cities of the United States and Europe; New York and London were the worst affected.

A continuing problem

During the early 20th century, improved living conditions in developed countries led to a decrease in the number of people with TB. With the arrival of effective treatments, doctors in these countries began to think that the days of TB were over. But in the 1980s, it became clear that TB was on the increase again in the United States and Europe, just as it was worldwide. It has now become a serious problem for the whole world.

This illustration of 17th-century slum life in England shows just how overcrowded some areas could be.

The Brontë sisters

Charlotte, Emily, and Anne Brontë were novelists who lived in England in the early 1800s. Their most famous books are Charlotte's *Jane Eyre* and Emily's *Wuthering Heights*. Like so many others at the time, the family was destroyed by TB. All three sisters, and their brother Branwell, died of TB as young adults. Charlotte was the last to die, at just 39 years old.

The spread of TB within the Brontë family was not unexpected since they lived closely together in a small, overcrowded room. Their father, who lived somewhat apart from his children, did not suffer from TB and lived to be 84!

TB treatment

For centuries there were no effective treatments for TB. To treat a disease, doctors first have to understand it. It is only in the last 300 years that the facts about TB have gradually become known.

Sanatoriums

As doctors began to understand more about TB, they tried a variety of treatments. Sanatoriums were special hospitals in the countryside where patients were made to rest and given good, nutritious food. This helped to strengthen the body's immune system. It also isolated the patients so that they could not spread TB. Many sanatoriums closed for good in the 1950s. They were no longer needed after the introduction of antibiotics.

Surgery

At the end of the 19th century, surgeons started performing various surgical operations on the lungs to help people with TB. The main goal was to rest the lungs by collapsing parts of them. These rather drastic procedures did actually give relief to some people with TB at a time when there were very few other options. But they did not provide a cure.

Robert Koch, a famous scientist, studied the problem of TB in the late 19th century.

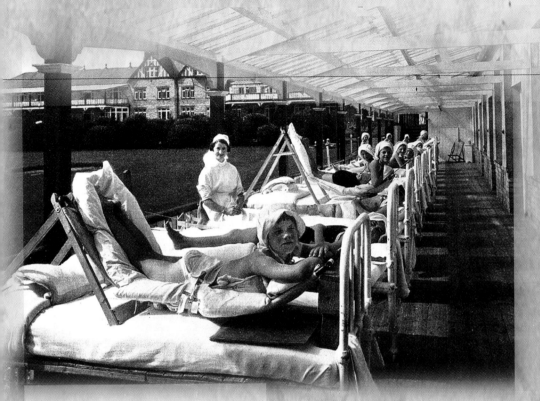

Antibiotics and vaccines

In 1944 scientists finally developed a medicine to treat TB. The medicine, an antibiotic called streptomycin, was developed in the United States. There were some early problems when doctors found that streptomycin had serious side effects. But newer and safer medicines soon appeared and TB became a curable disease.

A vaccine against TB was developed in France and first given to humans in 1921. It did not protect everyone who received it. However, when widespread vaccination was first introduced in 1954, the vaccine probably helped to reduce the numbers of cases of TB in countries such as the United Kingdom.

Patients in sanatoriums often slept on balconies in the open air.

Early milestones in knowledge of TB

- In 1679, Sylvius, a doctor in Holland, described tubercles, the small clumps of infected tissue found in the body in TB. This is where the name tuberculosis comes from.
- In 1720, Benjamin Marten, an English doctor, suggested that TB might be caused by "wonderfully minute living creatures" – what we know now to be bacteria.
- In 1882, TB bacteria were first seen by Robert Koch. He invented a special way of staining the TB bacteria so that they could be seen under a microscope.

What Is Tuberculosis?

Tuberculosis is caused by bacteria, tiny germs that are so small that even 1,000 of them laid end to end would still not be as long as a grain of rice. A number of different bacteria can cause TB, but all are members of a family called the Mycobacteria. The most common is *Mycobacterium tuberculosis*. Another, *Mycobacterium bovis*, comes from cows.

TB bacteria

The bacteria that cause TB can be seen only by using a microscope. The bacteria look like long, thin rods with rounded ends. Each one is a separate living organism. All it needs is a tiny area of warm human tissue in which to grow and multiply to make more bacteria.

Many types of bacteria can cause diseases in humans, but TB bacteria are different because they have an unusually strong cell wall, or protective skin. Most bacteria are killed when they are eaten by macrophages – some of the body's special defense cells. But the TB bacterium's tough cell wall means it survives and infects the macrophage by living and growing inside it.

The pathology of TB

Pathology is what happens in the cells and tissues of the body during a disease. The pathology of TB has fascinated doctors and scientists for many years.

When TB bacteria first start an infection, macrophages come to destroy them. When the macrophages then become infected, the body tries something else. Other types of defense cells arrive to surround the area of infection, forming a clump of cells known as a tubercle. These cells help kill the bacteria, and also build a wall around the area so that the infection cannot spread.

What happens next depends mainly upon how fit and healthy the infected person is. Often the defense cells win, and the TB bacteria die. Occasionally, the TB bacteria break out and spread to other parts of the body, or into the lungs to be coughed out. Sometimes the bacteria survive but are held captive by the defense cells, perhaps for many years. If in the future that person's resistance to disease is lowered for whatever reason, the TB bacteria may be able to break out and cause disease.

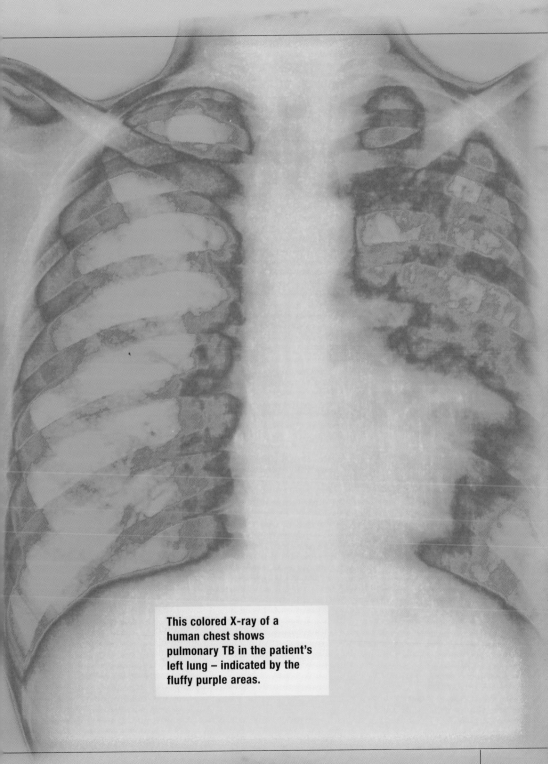

This colored X-ray of a human chest shows pulmonary TB in the patient's left lung – indicated by the fluffy purple areas.

Infection and disease

When talking about TB, it is important to realize the difference between TB infection and TB disease. With most bacteria, being infected means having the disease. But TB is different. Because TB bacteria are unusual, the way they cause disease is unusual, too. In many cases the bacteria do not cause disease until years after the infection begins.

TB infection

In TB infection a person carries dormant bacteria. The bacteria are held at bay by the body's strong defenses – the immune system. They are kept contained in areas such as the top of the lungs.

People with TB infection cannot pass TB to other people and so there is no danger to others. About one in ten of the people who have TB infection will go on

Close contact is safe if there is only TB infection, not disease.

❝My grandfather, who used to live with us, had TB. I must have caught it from him but that was several years ago!❞

(Gary, nineteen)

to develop TB disease at some time in their lives. Therefore, when people are diagnosed with this type of TB infection, their doctor may want to give them treatment to kill the dormant bacteria.

TB disease

TB disease is also known as active TB. This occurs when the bacteria break out and infect the surrounding tissues because the body's defenses are no longer strong enough to contain them. This is most likely to happen within five years of the initial infection, but may be many years later. Someone with TB disease affecting the lungs may pass on the bacteria to others who are living in close contact.

TB infection can develop into disease if the immune system is weakened by things such as drug abuse.

The reactivation of TB

TB can be reactivated by a wide range of things, in fact by just about anything that weakens the immune system of the body. Possible factors include:

- other illnesses, such as diabetes or some cancers
- malnutrition (not enough food)
- alcoholism
- HIV infection
- drug abuse
- some medicines such as steroids, and those that are used to suppress the immune system after organ transplants
- old age.

Effects on the body

Primary TB infection

Primary TB occurs when a person first becomes infected by TB bacteria they have inhaled into the lungs. The bacteria multiply and spread to the lymph glands in the middle of the chest. However, if the person (often a child) is fairly healthy, the bacteria are killed or become inactive after only a mild illness, or perhaps no illness at all. Very often, primary TB leads to serious disease, especially if the person has a weak immune system, such as in someone with HIV infection.

Secondary TB infection

Secondary TB infection occurs when a person is already carrying some inactive bacteria in the body and the body's defenses become weakened. This secondary infection can happen in many places in the body, such as the brain, the lymph glands, and the bones. The most common site is the lungs, when it is known as pulmonary TB.

Pulmonary TB

Pulmonary means "of the lungs." Pulmonary TB usually affects the upper parts of the lungs, and large cavities (holes) are eaten away by the disease. When the cavities enlarge to include one of the main air passages of the lungs, the bronchi, large numbers of bacteria may be released with each cough. Then TB becomes contagious. Pulmonary TB, if not treated, destroys the lung tissues and causes death.

Coughing is the main visible symptom of pulmonary TB.

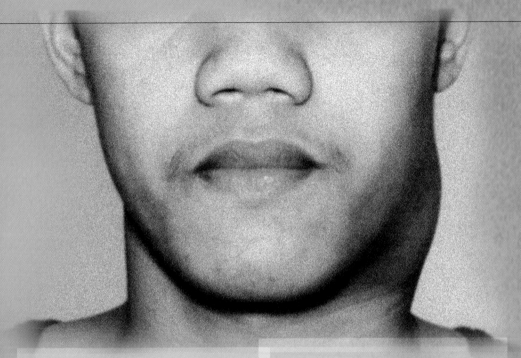

The rest of the body

TB in other parts of the body is much more common in children than in adults. Possible sites of infection include:

- lymph glands – small clumps of tissue found throughout the body that form part of the immune system. Swelling of the glands in the neck was once known as scrofula.
- bones and joints – TB of the vertebrae, or bones in the spine, was once called Pott's Disease.
- TB meningitis – this TB infection of the brain and surrounding tissues is rare but is often fatal.

TB can infect the lymph nodes of the neck, causing the disease once known as scrofula.

- urinary and reproductive tracts – this may include the womb in women. In some cases, the infection may even keep women from having babies. Bladder TB can occur in both men and women.
- miliary TB – this rare condition occurs when many body parts are infected at once after the bacteria first get into the bloodstream. It is often fatal.

Symptoms of TB

When someone first catches TB, the person may not feel ill at all or may feel slightly ill. He or she may just think they have the flu. It is later, when the bacteria break out to cause secondary TB, that the unpleasant illness begins.

In most cases of TB, the lungs are affected. Usually, one of the first things that a person notices is a cough. This is often worse in the mornings and can go on and on for many weeks. Phlegm, or spit, may be coughed up. After a while blood may also be coughed up from all the damage that the infection is causing in the lungs.

Malaise

As the disease takes hold, the sufferer will gradually feel more and more unwell, a feeling that doctors call malaise. There may be episodes of fever – raised temperature – especially at night. The person with TB may wake up to find the sheets wet with sweat.

TB in children

Children are more likely than adults to catch TB but less likely to have the obvious symptoms. It is also difficult to get a good sample of phlegm from children, since they usually swallow it instead of coughing it up. This means that it can be very difficult to diagnose TB in children.

Infants and babies under the age of four are more likely than adults to get TB in sites other than the lungs, such as the brain. For some reason the TB bacteria tend to be spread throughout the body in the bloodstream more easily in this young age group.

A person with TB may lose a lot of weight, since energy is used to fight the disease and there is little appetite for eating. Without treatment, the symptoms get worse and worse, and the lungs become severely damaged. The person will waste away and probably die as the body loses its fight against the invading bacteria. But with treatment it is usually possible to make a full recovery.

❝When I started getting ill, I lost lots of weight and kept coughing all the time. Eventually my mom nagged me to see the doctor.❞

(Gary, nineteen)

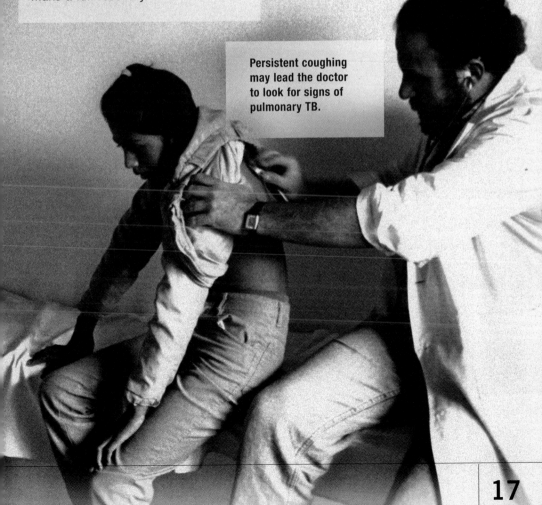

Persistent coughing may lead the doctor to look for signs of pulmonary TB.

How Is TB Spread?

TB is spread through the air, like the common cold. People with active TB of the lungs release bacteria into the air mainly when they cough, but also when they sneeze, sing, or even laugh. The bacteria can then be breathed in by another person, who may also become infected.

There are some important things to remember about the spread of TB:

- Not everyone who has TB can spread it to others. Those with active TB of the lungs, known as open TB, are most likely to pass it on.
- People with TB infection (carrying inactive TB bacteria) are not infectious.
- It is not easy to catch TB. There usually has to be close contact for quite a long time (eight hours or more).
- TB is not spread by touching or sharing utensils, or by casual contact.
- On average, someone with open TB will infect ten to fifteen people per year.
- Someone with TB will usually stop being infectious roughly two weeks after starting antibiotic treatment.

- Children with TB do not usually infect others, perhaps because their coughs are not forceful enough to fill the air with bacteria.

Bovine TB

Bovine TB infects cattle (see pages 26–27). Humans can catch it through the air and also by consuming infected milk or meat. It is extremely rare to catch bovine TB in developed countries because cattle are tested for the disease, and all milk is pasteurized – heated to kill bacteria.

"Someone in the world is infected with TB every second."

(The World Health Organization, 2002)

Mandy's story

Mandy, eighteen, lives in Newcastle, United Kingdom. She began to feel sick one summer, and lost over 40 pounds (19 kilograms) during the next five months. She saw her family doctor when she developed a cough, but it was another few months before TB was diagnosed. Everyone was shocked.

Mandy had to tell the TB control nurse about all the people she had been in close contact with over the previous months. This included her neighbor's young children, whom she had often looked after. Mandy remembers, "I felt really sorry when the little kids I had been babysitting had to take medicine to stop them from getting TB from me." Luckily, they were all fine, and Mandy is allowed to babysit them again now that she has been treated.

Who Is Affected by TB?

TB is very common. Over two million people a year die from it and another eight million become sick. These figures are increasing every year. TB is most common in countries without a modern healthcare system and with poorer standards of living – what are often called developing countries. However, TB is also present in many of the world's richest countries. In many cases, the numbers there are growing, too.

This is the current situation in some developed countries:

- In the United States, the number of people with TB fell steadily from the late 19th century to a low point of 22,000 in 1984. Rates then started to increase again. Measures taken to control this rise have brought the numbers down again, with only 15,000 new cases reported in 2002.
- The United Kingdom saw a large decrease in cases from the middle of the 19th century until the 1980s. Since then, the number of people with TB has increased steadily to the current figure of roughly 7,000 new cases a year. Two-fifths of cases are in London alone.

- Australia has one of the lowest rates of TB infection in the world, with just over 1,000 new cases a year.
- Australia's neighbor, New Zealand, also has a low rate, currently around 400 cases of TB every year. However, rates are increasing, especially in the cities.

Greenland

North America

South America

In all of these countries, a large proportion of the people with TB are immigrants and refugees from other countries that have a much higher rate of TB infection. TB is also much more common in the big cities than in the rural areas.

The rest of the world

TB is on the increase throughout the world, especially in Africa and Southeast Asia. The levels of TB infection are so high that, in 1993, the World Health Organization (WHO) declared that TB was a "global emergency." This was the first time that the WHO had made such a statement.

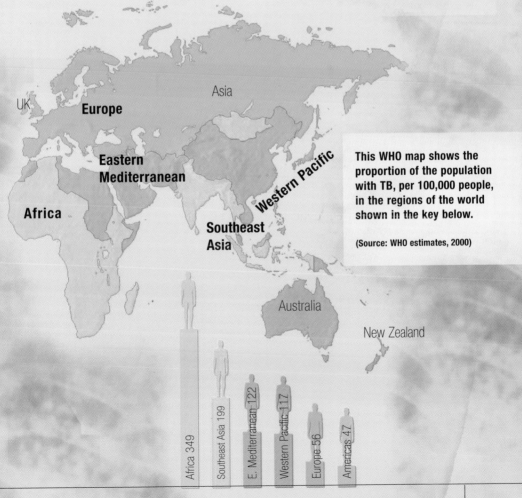

UK
Europe
Asia
Eastern
Mediterranean
Western Pacific
Africa
Southeast
Asia
Australia
New Zealand

This WHO map shows the proportion of the population with TB, per 100,000 people, in the regions of the world shown in the key below.

(Source: WHO estimates, 2000)

Africa 349
Southeast Asia 199
E. Mediterranean 122
Western Pacific 117
Europe 56
Americas 47

Who is at risk?

TB can infect anyone. It affects men and women of all ages and all ethnic groups. Poor and rich people get TB. However, some groups have a higher chance of catching it. This could be because they are more likely to be in close contact with someone with TB, or because they are more likely to catch TB if they come into contact with it.

> **"I wasn't surprised when my mother got TB – it's quite common among our old people. I didn't think that the children and I would get it, too."**
>
> **(Justine, 22, from an Aboriginal community in Australia)**

TB is a major health problem among some Aboriginal communities in Australia.

The people who have a greater risk of contracting TB include:

- people who have been in prolonged close contact with someone with TB infection; children and the very elderly are especially at risk in this situation because their immune systems are weaker
- people with other diseases – such as HIV infection, diabetes, or some cancers – that weaken the immune system
- those taking medicines, such as steroids, that weaken the immune system
- people born in areas of the world where TB is common, such as the Indian subcontinent and sub-Saharan Africa
- those who live in poor, overcrowded areas, especially in cities
- people in communities with high unemployment and poor living conditions, such as some of the indigenous (native) people of Australia and New Zealand
- homeless people
- people who have become dependent upon drugs or alcohol
- those suffering from malnutrition – meaning they do not have enough to eat to stay healthy
- prisoners, especially in countries such as Russia where prisons have very high rates of TB.

Being homeless like this man in the United Kingdom can mean a person is more likely to get TB.

The "shame" of TB

It is clear that, in many cases, TB is linked to poor standards of living. The association with poverty, homelessness, drug and alcohol abuse, prisons, and HIV infection have all led to a feeling that having TB is something to be ashamed of. For many people, having TB carries a stigma. They believe that having the disease marks them as a person who is less worthy of respect. This, of course, is totally untrue but it can cause problems when it comes to treatment. Sometimes a person finds it hard to admit that he or she, or someone in the family, has TB.

TB and HIV infection

TB has been around for thousands of years, while HIV, the human immunodeficiency virus that causes AIDS, emerged only a few decades ago. Yet today they make a deadly combination that causes millions of deaths around the world.

People who are infected with HIV have weakened immune systems, which makes them much more likely to get TB. They have a higher risk of catching TB from someone who is infectious and they are more likely to become ill with TB rather than just carrying inactive bacteria. While most people who catch TB for the first time do not develop the disease, those with HIV are quite likely to become ill almost immediately. In other cases, people with HIV become ill because the TB bacteria they were already carrying become active again.

Facts about HIV and TB

An estimated eleven million people around the world have both HIV and TB infection; the majority of them are in Africa.

- TB is the most common single cause of death worldwide in people with HIV. In the worst affected countries, half of all people with HIV die of TB.
- Sometimes the medicines given for HIV infection react badly with those given for TB. Doctors need to be very careful about what they prescribe and they need to check their patients regularly.
- Although there is a vaccine against TB – the BCG – this cannot be given to people with HIV since it can make them ill.
- If someone is infected with inactive TB, they have a ten percent chance of getting TB disease at some time during their life. If they have HIV infection too, then the likelihood increases by ten percent every year of their life.
- As HIV infection spreads throughout the developing world, the numbers of people with TB are bound to increase dramatically.

Unusual TB bacteria

As well as the most common TB bacteria (*Mycobacterium tuberculosis* and *Mycobacterium bovis*), other types of bacteria from the same family can cause TB. These are known as atypical TB bacteria, which means that they are not the usual type. These bacteria do not usually cause disease in healthy people but may infect people with HIV because of their weak immune systems.

This patient with AIDS in Uganda is also at high risk of getting TB.

The Animal Connection

Many animals can get TB, even lions! Perhaps the most important to humans are cattle. TB in cattle is caused by bacteria very similar to those that cause human TB. The disease is known as bovine TB (*bovine* means "to do with cows"). It damages their lungs just like it does in humans. Despite its name, bovine TB can also infect humans, causing a disease very similar to human TB.

Bovine TB was once fairly common in humans. The bacteria could be passed to humans who drank milk from an infected cow or worked closely with infected cows in a closed barn. In the early 1900s, in some countries such as the United States and United Kingdom, as many as one in three cows were infected.

Today, it is very unusual for someone in a developed country to catch bovine TB. All milk is now pasteurized – treated by heating it to kill off any bacteria that may be present, which includes the bovine TB bacteria. Bovine TB is also now extremely rare in cattle because for years many governments have taken action to test all cows and kill any that are infected. (Vaccination or treatment would be too costly.)

Most herds of cattle are free of TB in the United States and United Kingdom. In Australia, bovine TB seems to have been eliminated altogether.

Other animal carriers

Bovine TB bacteria are widespread, and can infect almost any mammal. This can be a problem for human health because cows can become infected by other animals and then pass the disease on to humans.

Some small mammals have been identified as passing TB to cows, including opossums in the United States and badgers in the United Kingdom. Governments have tried to reduce the number of cases of bovine TB by killing large numbers of these animals. In the United Kingdom, for example, an estimated 30,000 badgers have been killed in the last 30 years. Many people do not agree that badgers have been giving TB to cows and believe they should not be killed. Scientific studies are being carried out to determine the truth.

Cows were once a major source of TB in humans.

Living with Tuberculosis

The developing world

Rates of TB infection are very high in many developing countries. Even without tuberculosis, life can be extremely difficult in these places. Many people struggle to make a living. When TB is added to the equation, life becomes harder still – for the individual, the community, and the country as a whole.

Women and children

In most developing countries, women are responsible for the day-to-day care of children. When young women become ill and die of TB, their children may be left without anyone to care for them. Over 250,000 children die each year from TB, and the lives of many others are affected by the disease. In India alone, over 300,000 children are taken out of school each year to help their families cope with the effects of TB. These children do not then receive the education they need to improve their lives in the future.

School children study in Ghana. Schooling is often interrupted if there is TB in the family.

"TB is the single biggest killer of young women in the world, taking the lives of 750,000 each year."

(Kul Gautam, deputy executive director, UNICEF, 2000)

The local economy

If many people within a community have TB, it is difficult for them to rise out of poverty. When they have to buy medicines, or miss work to visit doctors, people earn less money to spend in local stores. They produce fewer goods for others to buy, so in the end the entire community is affected. Where TB is widespread, the whole country suffers. People with the disease cannot work to help the economy, but instead have to be supported by the country as a whole.

Eastern Europe

Although not classed as developing countries, many parts of the former Soviet Union have TB rates similar to those of countries such as India. This is mainly due to the disruption caused by the breakdown of Communist rule in the 1990s, which left the economy and welfare system in a disorganized state.

In Russia, Bulgaria, and Romania, cases of TB have been rising dramatically in the last ten years, mainly due to the steep rise in cases of HIV infection. In Kazakhstan, teenagers in particular have been affected. The re-emergence of TB in these countries adds to the many economic and social problems they have been facing during the restructuring of this region of the world.

These Chechen women in a refugee camp in eastern Europe are being checked for illness, including TB.

Deepa's story

Deepa, age fourteen, lives with her family in Delhi, a large city in India. They moved there from the countryside two years ago to look for work. Deepa, her parents, and her three younger sisters live in a one-room shack. She does not go to school any more. Her parents need her at home so that they can go out to work. She helps by looking after the younger children while her mother, Jaydevi, goes out to work as a cleaner.

Deepa suspected she had TB when she noticed how badly she was coughing when she got up each morning. She began to find it difficult to care for her sisters without frequent rests. When she saw blood in her spit one day, she grew frightened. Her parents had noticed that she was losing weight and had been worried about her for a few months. They now knew that the herbal medicine the local healer had sold them was not working and they would have to take Deepa to the hospital.

Seeking treatment

Deepa's father, Suresh, took her to the City Hospital. Although the treatment itself was free, this meant several days without Suresh's pay as they waited for doctor's appointments and tests. That week the whole family went hungry.

Deepa was given some medicines and took them every day as she had been told. After a few weeks she began to feel better and thought the TB had gone away. She did not go back to the hospital for more medicines because the family could not afford to lose another day's pay.

Ill again

Deepa has gradually become ill again and cannot look after her sisters or do housework properly. And while she is ill, Deepa is spreading the TB bacteria to all those she lives with. Her father will have to take her to the hospital again soon, and maybe this time there will be a happier ending for Deepa.

There are many other families like Deepa's, in India and throughout the rest of the developing world. They have little chance of improving their situation because their lives are damaged by TB. Hopefully one day, with better social conditions and more effective medicines, the burden of TB will be lifted and people like Deepa can live healthier and happier lives.

TB can make it difficult for many teenagers, such as this Indian girl, to look after their younger siblings.

The developed world

Although healthcare is better in developed countries, people who get TB still face many problems. One of the challenges is getting the correct diagnosis since many doctors believe that TB is no longer a problem in these countries. Sometimes this means that the disease has time to spread to others before it is treated.

If active TB is diagnosed, the patient usually has to stay away from other people for a couple of weeks until the antibiotics take effect. In this case, the

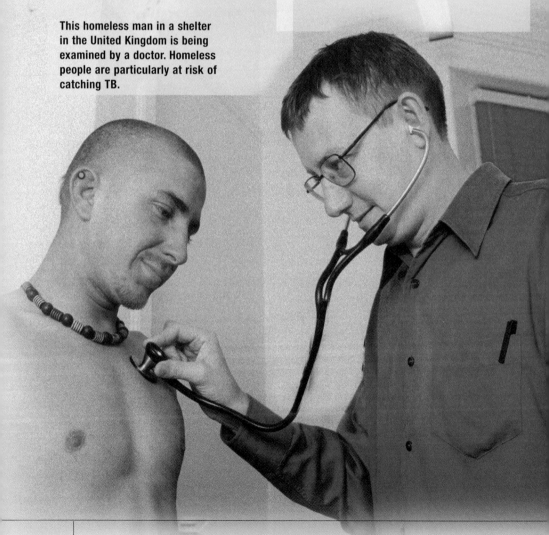

This homeless man in a shelter in the United Kingdom is being examined by a doctor. Homeless people are particularly at risk of catching TB.

person may have to stay in a hospital isolation room, which can be quite frightening. Being away from home can be difficult, especially if there are children to care for. For a child it will mean missing school, perhaps at a vital stage in their education.

Anxieties

People who have TB may worry about what other people will think of them. They may be nervous about losing their jobs because they need time off. Also, their employers might think that they will infect other workers. In this situation, a healthcare professional can help by providing the facts about TB and giving reassurance.

Everyone who has active TB will be asked about his or her contacts – the people the individual has been spending a lot of time with. It can be quite embarrassing for the person with TB when friends and family have to be checked, especially if those contacts then have to take medicines themselves. TB contact nurses try to protect people's privacy as much as possible.

Difficult lifestyles

Some people have real problems being diagnosed and treated for TB because of their difficult lifestyle. These include homeless people and drug abusers. Such people have a much higher than normal risk of getting TB. They may not realize they are ill and often have no family doctor to visit. Even if they are diagnosed, they may move from place to place, and might not stay in the same place for enough time to complete the long course of medicine needed for TB.

❝In the hospital they said I was infectious and put me in a room on my own. I got so fed up that I discharged myself.❞

(Gary, nineteen)

Diagnosis of TB

Diagnosing TB infection and disease can be quite difficult since TB can mimic a lot of other diseases.
The diagnosis involves:

- talking to the patient – asking about symptoms, and whether he or she has been in contact with TB
- skin testing
- a chest X-ray, to look for the telltale signs of TB chest infection
- examination of samples in the laboratory (see pages 36–37).

Skin testing

In skin testing, a tiny amount of liquid called tuberculin (an extract from TB bacteria) is injected under the skin of the forearm. There are two methods of doing this. The Heaf (or tine) test uses several small needles. The more accurate Mantoux test uses one larger needle.

The arm is then examined by an experienced healthcare professional two to three days later to see if there is any swelling and, if so, how much. The health worker uses his or her experience to decide whether the result is negative or positive. If there is no swelling, the result is negative, and there are probably no TB bacteria

A Heaf test is administered.

in the body. However, some people with HIV infection or reduced immunity may have a negative result even if they are infected with TB. Their immune system is not healthy and is unable to produce a reaction.

If the result is positive, the person may have TB infection. Further tests, such as a chest X-ray, are needed to reveal whether the infection is lying dormant (inactive) or whether there is active TB disease. A person who has had the BCG vaccination may also give a positive result.

"My doctor sent me for a chest X-ray and it was so abnormal that they took me into the hospital right away!"

(Mandy, eighteen)

When are skin tests performed?

Skin tests may be used when TB infection is suspected, or in some other situations:

- before giving the BCG vaccination; those with a negative test will need the vaccine to protect them from TB.
- for contacts of someone with active TB, to see if they have caught it themselves
- for people who have TB symptoms
- for people in high-risk groups, such as those with HIV infection, to see if they are carrying dormant TB bacteria.

On the left is an X-ray of a person with TB; you can see the damaged areas of the lungs. On the right is an X-ray of a healthy person.

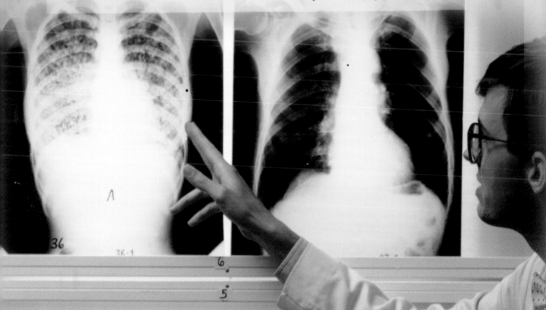

In the laboratory

A doctor or nurse may have a strong suspicion that a patient has TB. He or she will probably need the help of the microbiology laboratory to make a definite diagnosis. If a patient is suspected of having TB, a sample of the person's phlegm will be sent to the laboratory. In fact, many samples may be sent because there are often only a few TB bacteria present in each specimen.

If the TB infection is thought to be somewhere in the body other than the lungs, then different samples may be sent. These may include urine, a swab with pus on it, or even a piece of tissue that has been removed during an operation.

The microbiologist looks for TB bacteria using a microscope. This greatly magnifies the bacteria, by 200 times or more, so that they can be seen. To help spot the bacteria, the microbiologist first stains the sample with chemicals that make the bacteria appear red.

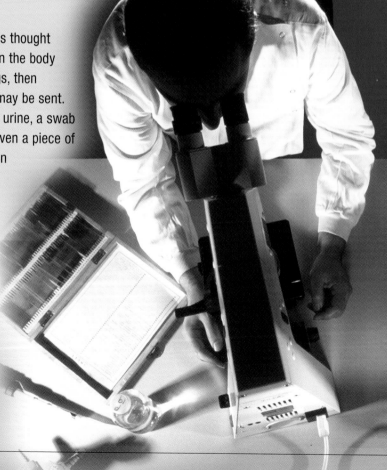

Next, the microbiologist tries to grow the TB bacteria. This is done by putting some of the specimen on special jelly called agar. It is placed in a warm incubator to help the bacteria grow. TB bacteria are much slower to multiply than most other bacteria. While most bacteria will multiply in a few days, TB bacteria may take six weeks or more! If TB bacteria are found, they may be sent to special reference laboratories to find out which strain, or type, they belong to. This sometimes helps health workers to discover where the patient became infected with TB.

Laboratory technicians may use optical microscopes such as these to check for TB bacteria in specimens or tissues.

Safety in the laboratory

There are strict rules about how specimens are handled so that people who work in laboratories do not catch TB from breathing in TB bacteria.

- Specimens are handled inside special safety cabinets that have an extractor fan to pull the bacteria away from the microbiologist's face.
- The cabinets are usually inside separate rooms that are used only for this purpose. This is to prevent other people from approaching too closely.
- All staff who work in these laboratories are vaccinated against TB (see page 38–39).

Vaccination

Preventing TB is easier than curing it. There is a vaccine for TB, called the BCG. It is believed to be the most widely used vaccine in the world today. The vaccine contains living bacteria, which are a weakened form of TB bacteria. They are too weak to cause disease, but are strong enough to stimulate the immune system against TB.

How good is the BCG?

Unfortunately, compared to most other vaccines, the BCG is not very effective. What effect it does have wears off after about fifteen years. At best, it protects approximately 80 percent of those who receive it.

Some people doubt that the vaccine helps at all. However, the BCG definitely seems to be effective in preventing extrapulmonary TB (disease outside the lungs), which is more common in children. Giving the vaccine to children at risk from TB infection helps protect them from the serious consequences of the spread of TB bacteria throughout the body.

This colored section of the BCG vaccine has been greatly magnified. The vaccine, shown in red, is infecting a white blood cell, which is colored green.

This Maori girl in New Zealand will receive the BCG vaccine.

"I'd had the BCG injection at school so I was really surprised when they said I'd caught TB."

(Joe, eighteen)

Who gets vaccinated?

Each country that uses the BCG has its own rules about who is given the vaccine. In developed countries, these people usually include:

- healthcare workers or others who may come into regular contact with people with TB
- babies born to families who have come from an area with a high rate of TB (such as India)
- babies from groups who are known to have a higher rate of TB, such as the Aboriginal people of Australia and the Maoris of New Zealand.

In the United States, the vaccine is rarely administered, and only to high-risk groups. Doctors do not believe the rates of TB are high enough to justify widespread vaccination. In the United Kingdom, most young teenagers are offered the BCG vaccine.

For the vaccine to work, the body must be healthy. In countries where many people find it hard to get enough food and where the general living conditions are poor, the BCG vaccine does not work well. Vaccination with BCG is not really the answer to the problem of TB throughout the world.

Treatment of TB

TB is almost completely curable if treated correctly. Since it is a bacterial infection, TB is treated with specific anti-TB antibiotics – medicines that kill bacteria. TB is an unusual disease in that it takes a long time to treat – many months instead of the five to ten days needed for most other bacteria. This is partly because TB bacteria can lie deeply hidden within the body's tissues. The type of antibiotic treatment taken depends upon whether the person in question has dormant TB infection or active TB disease.

Treatment of infection

People with TB infection are not sick. They carry the TB bacteria within their bodies but these bacteria are kept under control by the immune system. Even though there is no illness, in some cases it is worthwhile having preventive treatment to kill these bacteria because they might later cause disease. The usual treatment for TB infection is the antibiotic isoniazid, taken as a daily tablet for six to nine months.

Treatment of disease

Unlike the situation years ago, when many people died or had to spend years in special hospitals, TB disease can now be treated effectively with antibiotics. The treatment consists of a combination of three or four medicines – the most common being isoniazid, rifampicin, pyrazinamide, and ethambutol – taken for at least six months.

As with all antibiotics it is extremely important that the entire course is taken, even if the person feels absolutely fine again. This is to make sure that every single one of the bacteria is killed so that the disease will not come back again.

A small boy in Argentina taking medicine for TB. He will need to take it for many months.

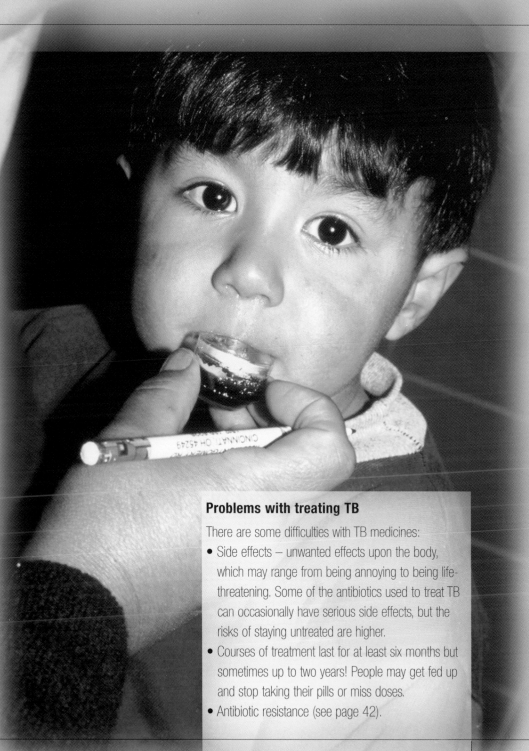

Problems with treating TB

There are some difficulties with TB medicines:

- Side effects – unwanted effects upon the body, which may range from being annoying to being life-threatening. Some of the antibiotics used to treat TB can occasionally have serious side effects, but the risks of staying untreated are higher.
- Courses of treatment last for at least six months but sometimes up to two years! People may get fed up and stop taking their pills or miss doses.
- Antibiotic resistance (see page 42).

Antibiotic resistance

Streptomycin, the first effective medicine against TB, was introduced in the 1940s. Many people thought that TB would be wiped out. However, it soon became clear that the TB bacteria could change to become resistant to this antibiotic – that is, the medicine would no longer kill them. This can happen with most bacteria but is more likely in TB. The antibiotics have to be given for a long period and the bacteria have more time to adapt.

Doctors realized that in order to stop resistance from developing, they had to give more than one antibiotic. Today, the treatment for TB usually includes three or four medicines, at least for the first few months.

Multi-drug resistant TB

Multi-drug resistant TB is the name given to TB bacteria that have become resistant to two or more of the main anti-TB medicines. This is becoming a serious problem in some parts of the world, especially in developing countries and some parts of eastern Europe.

TB bacteria become multi-resistant when people with TB do not take their medicines correctly, or when the wrong combinations of medicines have been prescribed to them. Multi-resistant TB is much harder to treat than normal TB because the medicines that have to be used in these cases (the second-line, or backup medicines) are not as effective as the first-choice medicines. Also, it costs roughly 100 times as much to treat than normal TB. This causes real difficulties in poorer countries.

❝Do I really have to take all these medicines? Surely one is enough.❞

(Cassie, fifteen, upon finding out she needed to take several drugs)

Directly Observed Therapy

Since the early 1990s, the World Health Organization has been promoting Directly Observed Therapy (DOT) as the best way of treating TB and preventing multi-resistance. This method includes a number of features. Perhaps the most valuable is that a trained healthcare worker actually watches the patient take the medicines he or she needs. This can be done at a clinic or even at the person's home or place of work. With this encouragement and support, the patient usually finishes the course of treatment correctly and is cured of TB, leaving no chance for multi-resistant bacteria to develop.

The DOT method of treatment is believed to be so important that the theme selected for World TB Day (on March 24, 2003) was "DOT cured me – it will cure you too!"

Here, a nurse supervises a patient taking the DOT treatment in South Africa.

Why Is TB Still a Problem?

TB is now almost completely curable and the antibiotics needed are mostly cheap and widely available. Why then is TB still a problem in the world today? Many factors are involved here.

A moving population

In many developing countries, the population increases year after year. As the number of people in a country rises, there tends to be movement away from the countryside and into cities. The result is often the growth of cramped, overcrowded slum communities within the cities, where TB can thrive.

In some parts of the developing world, large numbers of refugees flee their own country to escape war or famine. Often they gather in refugee camps, which are also very overcrowded communities.

With increased conflict in the world, more people from the countries with the greatest problems try to move to developed countries. They often come from countries with high levels of TB and may carry the infection themselves. More than half of the cases of TB in developed countries are found within immigrant or refugee communities.

"I was ill when I arrived in England with my family. But we didn't know that it was TB until I had some tests at the hospital."

(Ho, thirteen, an immigrant to the United Kingdom from Southeast Asia)

Poor healthcare

To treat TB correctly, and to prevent its spread within the community, a well-organized healthcare service is needed. Many countries cannot afford this. In some cases, inadequate treatment leads to multi-drug resistant TB, which just adds to the problem.

The number of people worldwide who are infected with HIV is increasing dramatically, especially in developing countries. In areas with HIV infection, TB is much more likely to cause disease and spread to others.

TB can thrive in crowded refugee camps, such as this one in Kosovo in the late 1990s.

Inadequate research

Many healthcare workers believe that not enough has been done to develop new methods of detection and treatment for TB. Skin testing is time consuming, expensive, and sometimes difficult to interpret. There is still no simple blood test for TB. New medicines are usually developed by commercial (profit-making) companies. Most people who have TB live in poorer countries and cannot afford to pay much for their medicines. Some people believe that if TB were more common in wealthier countries, better treatments would have become available by now.

TB and the Law

In many countries, a doctor who diagnoses TB in a patient must, by law, inform the health authorities. This is to allow measures to be taken to stop TB from spreading to others and to find out more information about where TB is occurring.

Contact tracing

Every person who has come into close contact with a case of active TB should be checked out to see if he or she has caught the disease. In many places, there are special TB contact nurses whose job it is to find these contacts. The nurse will look for those who have been living or working closely with the person with TB. These people will then be visited and tested to see if they have signs of infection.

Compulsory detention

Most people with TB understand that they must take their medicines and stay inside for a few weeks while these take effect. In some cases, people may be offered food vouchers or better housing to encourage them to take their medicines correctly.

However, some people do not agree to take medicine or stay away from others. In some countries, there are laws that allow authorities to hold a person with active TB against his or her will in a safe place, such as a hospital. This loss of freedom is unfortunate and some people may think it is wrong. But detention is only used as a last resort to protect other people from TB.

A TB contact nurse will meet with people who might be at risk of TB, just as this nurse is talking to her patient.

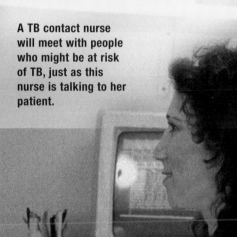

Detention in New York

In 1993, after infection rates for TB began to rise again in the United States, New York City reintroduced an old law that allowed people with this disease to be detained in a hospital.

Alberto Plassey, a man who had been suffering from active TB for several years, had not been cured because he found it too difficult to take his medicines properly. In 1998 he felt sick and visited one of the city's hospitals. To his surprise, he was then taken to a special detention hospital, where he remained under guard for two years. Finally, in the spring of 2000, he walked free – cured of TB and no longer a health threat to those around him.

❝Why can't I go out? I don't want to stay in. I'm going to see my friends and you can't stop me.❞

(Jim, eighteen, who had been told to remain at home while taking TB medicines)

How Can Modern Science Help?

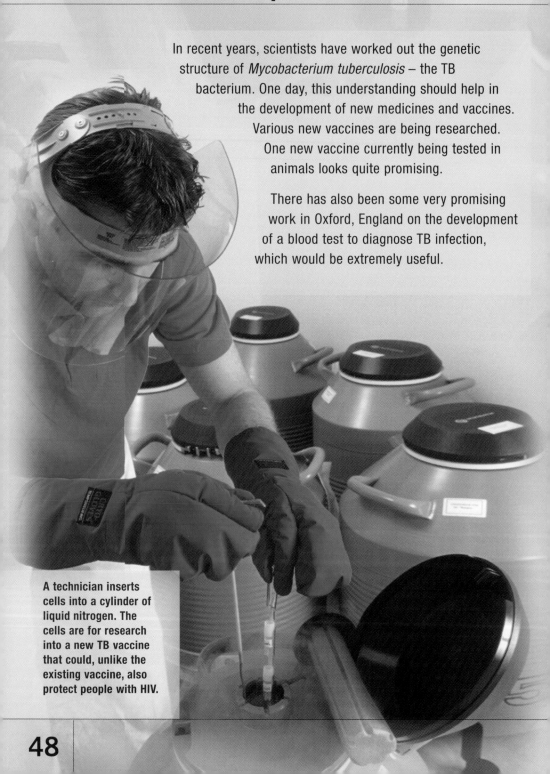

In recent years, scientists have worked out the genetic structure of *Mycobacterium tuberculosis* – the TB bacterium. One day, this understanding should help in the development of new medicines and vaccines. Various new vaccines are being researched. One new vaccine currently being tested in animals looks quite promising.

There has also been some very promising work in Oxford, England on the development of a blood test to diagnose TB infection, which would be extremely useful.

A technician inserts cells into a cylinder of liquid nitrogen. The cells are for research into a new TB vaccine that could, unlike the existing vaccine, also protect people with HIV.

New medicines

There is a great need for new medicines that will work more quickly than the current ones. Shorter courses would be easier to finish. Some new medicines have appeared already – rifapentine, for example, was approved for use in TB in 1999. Other potential new medicines are being tested and will take their place in the fight against TB.

International co-operation

Although modern science has a lot to offer in the treatment of TB, the control of this disease in the world as a whole will only be achieved through international support and co-operation. Those countries with greater resources need to help their poorer neighbors, for the benefit of all.

To help achieve this, a number of organizations have been created over recent years:

- The Global Alliance for TB Drug Development is an international not-for-profit enterprise that is actively looking for better anti-TB medicines.
- The Global Partnership to Stop TB works with governments, research institutions, and private companies to help find practical solutions to the worldwide problem of TB. Associated with this group is the Global TB Drug Facility, which aims to provide low-price TB medicines to the poorest countries in the world.
- The Global Fund to Fight AIDS, Tuberculosis, and Malaria is a new organization that collects money to fight these three diseases that are causing so many deaths around the world.

"Two million people continue to die every year from a disease that has been treatable and preventable for over half a century. Such a situation is unjust and incomprehensible."

(The Global Partnership to Stop TB, 2000)

TB – A Challenge for the Future

TB poses a huge challenge. With the seemingly unstoppable rise of HIV infection and the increase in world population, the conditions are rife for TB to continue to cause more death and disease than any other infection.

People watch the TV in horror when there is a plane crash or an earthquake that kills hundreds. It is right to be shocked at such loss of life. Yet each day, roughly 6,000 people die of TB – the equivalent of 20 major plane crashes. Almost all of these deaths could be prevented through the use of simple medicines that cost very little.

❝...between 2002 and 2020, approximately 1,000 million people will be newly infected, over 150 million people will get sick, and 36 million will die of TB – if control is not further strengthened.❞

(The World Health Organization)

The director of the World Health Organization, Lee Jong-Wook (left), knows what an important task lies ahead to control TB.

Simple solutions

With increasing numbers of cases in their own countries, the developed world has started to wake up to the fact that something needs to be done about TB. People in developing countries want to help themselves but they need the support and resources of richer nations.

Simple measures, such as improved living conditions and good basic healthcare, will help to prevent TB. Introduction of the DOT regime in every developing country promises to reduce numbers of TB cases dramatically. Modern research to find a better, more effective vaccine and newer medicines that act more quickly will then provide the final steps in the elimination of this disease.

Signs of hope

There are some signs of hope. Several countries in Asia, including some poorer countries such as Cambodia and Vietnam, are well on their way to effectively controlling TB. Some richer countries, such as the United Stated, have managed to stop the increase in cases and are starting to see a decrease.

These demonstrators in India are trying to increase the awareness of TB in their community.

With co-operation between the countries of the world, it should eventually be possible to control TB, and hopefully one day to eliminate it altogether from human society.

Information and Advice

Around the world, a number of organizations are trying to increase awareness of the growing problem of TB, and are campaigning for better treatments. Many of these provide up-to-date information about TB through fact sheets and websites.

Contacts

Global Alliance for TB Drug Development
59 John Street, Suite 800
New York, NY 10038
Tel: 1 (212) 227-7540
Fax: 1 (212) 227-7541
Website: www.tballiance.org
A not-for-profit organization that works to help speed up the discovery of faster-acting and affordable drugs for TB.

The New Jersey Medical School National Tuberculosis Center
Website: www.umdnj.edu/ntbcweb
This site has a lot of very straightforward information about TB as well as an extensive list of useful links to other TB sites.

The Global Partnership to Stop Tuberculosis
Website: www.stoptb.org
An international organization that works with governments, research institutions and private companies to help find practical solutions to the worldwide problem of TB.

International Union against Tuberculosis and Lung Disease
68 Boulevard Saint Michel
75006 Paris, France
Tel: (33) 1 44 320360
Fax: (33) 1 43 299087
Website: www.iuatld.org
The IUATLD has as its mission the prevention and control of tuberculosis and lung disease, as well as related health problems, on a worldwide basis, with a particular emphasis on low income countries. The site provides some downloadable fact sheets on TB and other causes of lung disease.

World Health Organization
WHO Headquarters
TWebsite: www.who.int
The World Health Organization is the United Nations specialized agency for health, and is run by representatives from 192 countries. It exists to work for good health for people everywhere.

More Books to Read

Cohen, Joel H. *Tuberculosis*. Farmington Hills, Mich.: Gale Group, 2002.

Finer, Kim. *Tuberculosis.* Broomall, PA.: Cheslea House Publishing, 2003.

Silverstein, Alvin and Silverstein, Virgina. *Tuberculosis.* Berkeley Heights , NJ: Enslow Publishers, 1994.

Sliverstein, Alvin. *What Are Germs?* Danbury, CT.: Scholastic Library Publishing, 2002.

Yancey, Diane. *Tuberculosis.* Breckenridge, CO; Twenty-first Century Books, 2001.

Glossary

Aboriginal people
people already living in Australia when European settlers arrived

active TB
actual illness caused by TB that can often be caught by others

antibiotic resistance
ability of a bacterium to survive in the presence of an antibiotic

antibiotics
medicines that kill bacteria

bacteria
tiny living organisms that can only be seen under a microscope; some bacteria, including the ones that cause TB, cause disease

BCG
stands for Bacille Calmette-Guerin and is the vaccination used against TB

bovine TB
form of TB that affects cows (*bovine* means "to do with cows")

contagious
carrying a disease that can be passed on to others

developed country
usually a rich country, with many industries and a complex economic system

developing country
usually a poor country that is trying to make its industry and economic system more advanced

Directly Observed Therapy (DOT)
method of treating people with TB that involves a healthcare worker monitoring that each dose of medicine is taken properly

dormant
lying inactive, or sleeping

genetic structure
arrangement of the genes that control how a living thing develops

HIV (Human Immunodeficiency Virus) infection
viral infection that can lead to the condition known as AIDS; people who are infected with HIV are at a much higher risk of getting TB

immigrants
people who leave their country of origin and move to a new country to live

immune system
body's defense system, made up of various types of cells that can recognize and kill invading bacteria

isolation
act of keeping someone away from other people, such as in a separate room in a hospital or at home, to keep an infection such as TB from being passed on

lymph gland
small clump of tissue within the body that helps the immune system to catch and kill bacteria

macrophage
one of the types of defense cells in the body that works by destroying bacteria

meningitis
infection of the tissues around the brain

microbiology
study of micro-organisms – tiny living creatures – and how they affect the body

miliary TB
serious form of TB, found most often in young children and those with a damaged immune system, in which the bacteria have been carried throughout the body by the bloodstream

multi-drug resistant TB
form of TB in which the bacteria have become resistant to several different antibiotics at one time, making them very difficult to kill

Mycobacteria
family of bacteria to which TB belongs

Mycobacterium bovis
scientific name for the bacteria that cause TB in cows and other animals

Mycobacterium tuberculosis
scientific name for the bacteria that cause TB

open TB
active lung disease form of TB in which patients cough out TB bacteria that can then infect others

pasteurize
to kill bacteria by heating

phlegm
sticky mucus that is coughed up when someone has a lung infection (also known as sputum)

Pott's disease
TB of the bones of the spine

primary TB
first infection with TB bacteria, which often goes unnoticed but may give mild flu-like symptoms

pulmonary TB
TB disease of the lungs

pus
sticky, yellowish fluid that collects in sites of infection

reference laboratory
specialized laboratory that performs tests on bacteria

secondary TB
re-emergence of TB from its inactive form to cause disease

side effects
unwanted, and sometimes harmful, effects of a medicine

specimen
small quantity of blood, urine, or phlegm that is taken from a patient to be tested in a laboratory

staining
process of coloring a specimen (usually as a smear on a glass microscope slide) to highlight any bacteria

sub-Saharan Africa
countries in Africa that lie south of the Sahara desert

TB disease
condition in which the TB bacteria have broken out of their inactive state to cause disease within the body; a person with TB disease may pass it on to others

TB infection
condition in which TB bacteria lie inactive inside the body; a person with TB infection will not pass it on to others

tissues
mass of cells that form the different parts of the body

tubercles
clumps of cells that grow in response to the presence of TB bacteria and try to kill the infection

vaccine
medicine that is given, usually by injection, to a healthy individual in order to prevent the person from catching a particular infectious disease in the future

Index